W9-CHS-692

Animal
Gymnastics Stars

BY GAIL TERP

The Child's World®
childsworld.com

Published by The Child's World®
1980 Lookout Drive • Mankato, MN 56003-1705
800-599-READ • www.childsworld.com

Photographs ©: iStockphoto, cover, 1, 9; Anne McKinnell/All
Canada Photos/Glow Images, 5; Leonard Zhukovsky/Shutterstock
Images, 6; Fernando Frazão/Agência Brasil, 7; A. Whitmore
Photography/Shutterstock Images, 10, 20–21; Shutterstock
Images, 11; Christopher Gardiner/Shutterstock Images, 13, 21;
N.A. Finney/iStockphoto, 15; Jurgen & Christine Sohns/FLPA/
ImageBROKER RM/Glow Images, 17; Gudkov Andrey/Shutterstock
Images, 18, 20

ISBN 9781503820395
LCCN 2016960509

Printed in the United States of America
PA02341

ABOUT THE AUTHOR

Gail Terp is a retired elementary teacher who now writes for kids and beginning adult readers. Her books for kids cover history, science, animals, and biographies. When not reading and writing, she walks around looking for interesting stuff to write about. She lives in Upstate New York.

Contents

CHAPTER 1

Gymnastics Stars

The animal world is full of gymnasts. These athletes move **gracefully** through trees. They leap away from danger. They **balance** on narrow places.

Gymnastics is a difficult sport. Gymnasts leap high in the air. While up there, they do flips and twists. Then, they land neatly on their feet.

To score well in competitions, human gymnasts must have difficult **routines**. They work from mats on the floor and on high bars. They also use a balance beam. This beam is only four inches (10 cm) wide. And still, the gymnasts leap, flip, and twist.

Cliffs serve as nature's balance beams.

Simone Biles's signature event is the floor routine.

Simone Biles is a gymnast. She leaps very high. She does flips in the air. She can twist in the air many times. Biles is strong and **flexible**. She has great balance. In the 2016 Summer Olympics, Biles won four gold medals. She earned them because her routines were very difficult.

Biles is a gymnastics star. Nature is also full of star gymnasts. Which animal would win the gold medal if this were an Olympic competition?

To find out, three animals will be compared. To decide which animal is the best, they will be judged in four areas. Is the animal strong? Does the animal move in flexible ways? Does the animal have great balance? Is the animal graceful? Who will be the winner? Time to compare!

ATHLETE PROFILE
NAME: Simone Biles
HEIGHT: 4.6 feet (142 cm)
WEIGHT: 105 pounds (48 kg)
RECORDS HELD: Gold Medals in floor, vault, all-around, and women's team

CHAPTER 2

Ace of the Treetops

Eastern gray squirrels are known for being quick. They run gracefully through the trees. They leap from branch to branch. The squirrels race along the thinnest branches.

Eastern gray squirrels live in forests. They also live in towns and cities. Most live in the United States and Canada. Eastern gray squirrels are also found in parts of Europe. Some build their homes in holes in tree trunks. Others make leafy nests high in trees. Eastern gray squirrels mostly eat nuts and fruits.

ANIMAL PROFILE
NAME: Eastern Gray Squirrel
LENGTH: 19 inches (48 cm), including tail
WEIGHT: 18 ounces (510 g)

Eastern gray squirrels venture out on pencil-thin branches to reach food.

Eastern gray squirrels can communicate by flicking their tails.

Eastern gray squirrels can leap great distances. They can jump 20 feet (6 m) from one tree branch to the next. They rarely fall while running along narrow branches.

But if they do, they land on their feet. Eastern gray squirrels also use their tails to help them balance.

On the ground, eastern gray squirrels can run up to 15 miles per hour (24 km/h). They can also do twists and flips.

Fun Fact

Eastern gray squirrels can swim. They swim with their heads up and tails flat on top of the water.

Eastern gray squirrels have little need for strength. When they hang onto things, their sharp, curved claws do most of the work. Plus, they can be very flexible. Their back feet can rotate 180 degrees around! Then they can run headfirst down trees.

Eastern gray squirrels are great at bending their bodies in order to reach food.

CHAPTER 3

Balance Expert

Mountain goats live on high mountains in North America. Most live on mountains more than 10,000 feet (3,048 m) high. They get around by climbing steep cliffs. They make long, graceful hops from rock to rock. To get to their food, they balance carefully on narrow ledges.

Mountain goats eat plants that grow between rocks. Few other animals live so high up. This keeps mountain goats safe from enemies.

ANIMAL PROFILE
NAME: Mountain Goat
HEIGHT: 3.6 feet (191 cm)
WEIGHT: 100 to 300 pounds (45 to 136 kg)

Mountain goats have rings on their horns that tell how old they are. The more rings, the older the goat!

Mountain goats have powerful front legs. These help pull the goats up cliffs that are nearly straight up and down. Their strong legs also help them slow down as they go down cliffs.

Mountain goats have hooves that help them balance. Each hoof has two toes. These toes can pinch together. This helps the goats hold onto a ledge while they eat. Plus, rough pads on the bottom of each foot help keep the goats from sliding.

Mountain goats are great leapers. They can jump 10 feet (3 m) from ledge to ledge. However, as gymnasts, mountain goats don't have a lot of flexibility. They can't do flips and twists.

Mountain goats will climb the sides of mountains just one day after being born!

CHAPTER 4

Leaping Master

Sifakas are a type of lemur. Lemurs are primates. Sifakas live only in Madagascar. This is an island nation off the coast of Africa. They live in forests. The sifaka mostly eats leaves, flowers, and fruit.

Sifakas have short arms but very strong, large legs. With them, they can leap more than 30 feet (9 m) from tree to tree. Unlike other lemurs, sifakas remain completely upright when they leap.

ATHLETE PROFILE
NAME: Sifaka
Height: 1.4 to 1.6 feet (41 to 46 cm)
TAIL LENGTH: 1.5 to 2 feet (.46 to .61 m)
WEIGHT: 7 to 13 pounds (3 to 6 kg)

Sifakas get their name from the unique call that they make.

The sideways leap sifakas make has been described as a dance-like movement.

Sifakas also have very long tails. They use their tails to balance while they jump. At times, sifakas are not quite facing the trees that they are jumping toward. To fix this, they turn in midair to make a perfect landing.

Sifakas live in groups. Family sizes can range from three to ten sifakas. They forage for food together during the day. Then they climb back up to their lofty home at night. Sifakas spend most of their time in trees. But they can also move gracefully on the ground. They stand tall on their legs and make sideways hops. To keep their balance, they raise their arms high.

Currently, the sifaka population is threatened. Much of their habitats are ruined by the destruction of forests.

Fun Fact

In sifaka families, the females are in charge. They get first choice in food and nesting sites.

CHAPTER 5

The Award Ceremony

GOLD MEDAL
Sifaka

SILVER MEDAL
Eastern Gray Squirrel

It's time to award the medals! The sifaka wins the gold medal! The sifaka keeps its balance in the trees and on the ground. The eastern gray squirrel can leap far, plus do flips and twists. This makes it the best choice for the silver medal. The mountain goat wins the bronze medal. Congratulations to the winners!

BRONZE MEDAL
Mountain Goat

Glossary

balance (BAL-uhns) Balance is the ability to remain steady and upright. The mountain goat keeps its balance as it leaps from rock to rock.

flexible (FLEK-suh-buhl) Something that is flexible is able to bend. Squirrels show they are flexible by quickly changing directions when running on trees.

gracefully (GRAYSS-ful-ee) When something is done gracefully, it is done beautifully and elegantly. Sifakas move gracefully through the trees.

routine (roo-TEEN) A routine is a part of a sports performance that is carefully worked out so it can be repeated. A gymnast will practice his or her routine many times.

To Learn More

In the Library

Leaf, Christina. *Gray Squirrels*.
Minneapolis, MN: Bellwether Media, 2015.

Magby, Meryl. *Mountain Goats*.
New York, NY: PowerKids Press, 2014.

Phillips, Dee. *Flying Lemur*.
New York, NY: Bearport Pub., 2014.

On the Web

Visit our Web site for links about animals that
are flexible: **childsworld.com/links**

Note to Parents, Teachers, and Librarians: We routinely verify our
Web links to make sure they are safe and active sites.
So encourage your readers to check them out!

Index